Dr. Da

INFLUENCE

How To Get It and Keep It

HB

Hamilton-Bruce

Orlando · Toronto

For forthcoming titles, workshops, and support materials, visit Dan Neundorf at www.drneundorf.com.

ISBN 13: 978-0-973-97843-8

ISBN 10: 973-397-8430

Printed in Canada

DEDICATION

This book is dedicated to those who love to learn.
It is one of the greatest gifts we are given
and get to give.

Norman,
Happy influence.
04/18

CONTENTS

INTRODUCTION

"There are two thoughts that often get lost in the discussion about being effective in building and using influence: Don't assume you have all the right answers—that's why a strong team is essential. And, above all, do the right thing—not only for business or economic impact, but also for social and philosophical implications. Ultimately, power is the ability to influence and facilitate change, and people naturally rally around leaders who do the right thing consistently."

Ralph Szygenda, former CIO of General Motors,
in *Optima Magazine*

As a hands-on executive coach for 25 years, I felt I was doing everything right. My clients were satisfied, their sales increased, and so did my referrals. But one day in 2007, I read a startling statement: *Poor relationships are the number-one factor in derailing success.* And it had the statistics to back it up. My practice changed on that day. I began to research everything I could find on the subject of relationships. I read voraciously—books, magazines, research reports. Gradually, I began to synthesize the research findings into my coaching sessions. Over time, I developed a systematic, practical approach to influencing others that worked and worked well. As my clients began to apply the approaches we discussed during our sessions, their relationships improved dramatically. They started to get more meetings, more time with their customers, and more "yes's." They were thrilled. So was I.

What happened next was amazing. The people my clients sought to influence actually *sought them out* and requested more time. They even wanted advice from my clients on issues far beyond their expertise. This posed a critical question: How could my clients support these people so their relationships with them could continue to evolve and strengthen? Thus began role system dynamics, a strategic system of changing relationships that are adaptable to any situation. Join with me now in investigating the relationship strategies that will influence others to change perspective and take you beyond "*Yes*."

Dr. Dan Neundorf

ABOUT THE AUTHOR

A pioneer in developing and facilitating cutting-edge management and leadership programs, Dr. Dan Neundorf is a dynamic communicator, elevating performance through the skills of coaching, counseling, and mentoring. His workshops and seminars have helped hundreds of individuals advance their careers and dramatically improved the management and productivity of companies and not-for-profits throughout North America.

President and lead trainer of Impact Training and Development Inc., in Canada, Dr. Neundorf holds a doctorate in education with a specialization in training and development from Northcentral University, where he is also a mentor. His earlier career includes launching a five-tier leadership development program for managers, directors, and executives; implementing a change-management model for human resources; launching web-based training systems and corporate intranets; and coordinating corporate training initiatives for global operations. His workshops in leadership and influence have earned such plaudits as "captured the minds and hearts of our people."

Contact Dr. Neundorf at www.drneundorf.com.

CHAPTER ONE

WHY PEOPLE CHANGE THEIR MINDS

Hannibal leveraged it to move elephants and men. Queen Victoria leveraged it to expand the British Empire. So did American Presidents Reagan ("Mr. Gorbachev—Tear down that wall!") and Kennedy ("Ich bin ein Berliner!"). What is influence? Can anyone use it? Can anyone learn it? Why is influence essential to doing business?

The answer is simple. It's the way to get buy-in of a product, service, idea, policy, or message—and to do that, you need a commitment. Although the AIDA model can be interpreted too strictly, advertisers, sales persons, and others usually follow it. It's a basic, step-by-step process to change someone's mind by first creating awareness, then interest, then desire—and finally to influence them to take action.

Influence is not an instrument but a response, and persuasion is a method of influence in action, an attempt to lead people to adopt a particular behavior, belief, or idea—or to change their minds. Social psychologists tell us that people process and interpret new information, accepting or rejecting it, based on whether it reinforces or contradicts their beliefs. In fact, people will hold on to some beliefs, even if false, because those beliefs allow them to function in their daily lives. For example, people in Japan still eat Japan-caught fish and Japan-grown produce even though the levels of radiation are known to be unacceptably high. Social cognition, a growing area of social psychology, tells us that people form impressions of others while they're interacting with them. In addition, all things being equal, people would rather buy from a person they know and like than from a stranger. And a favorite of compliance professionals: People are likelier to acquiesce in a decision, accept an idea, even buy a product or service if the outcome is easy to imagine and the possibility stands out in the mind as vivid and memorable.

You probably never thought of yourself as a "compliance professional," but you are. Marketer, sales person, advertiser, public relations strategist, business leader, politician or pollster—you have to be expert in gaining influence and using it. Your ability to craft successful relationships—and messages—is vital to getting work done and done right. To do that, you first have to understand the psychology and facets of influence. The need to do so is crucial: The pressure to produce results has never been greater. On both the organizational and career levels, competition is increasingly sharp and aggressive. Products and services are being commoditized with regularity. Technology and distance have created an interpersonal chasm that remains to be bridged, while oppressive governments are collapsing under the democratizing influence of social media. These are world phenomena, and the world is still reeling from a crippling economic crisis. Growth in recovery continues to be slower than anticipated, with the average GDP of even the most advanced OECD economies falling well below the levels of 2007. While most OECD governments deal with massive budget deficits, a dismal debt-to-income ratio, and intolerably high unemployment—double-digit in some countries, the emerging economies of China and India continue to forge ahead. Meanwhile, analysts anxiously study the foreign currency markets and the slow growth in international trade.

"The vast majority of today's [global] crises," says Joseph Grenny in a *Bloomberg Businessweek* special report, "are the natural consequences of ineffective or misdirected influence. Leaders are responsible for intelligently and ethically influencing behavior in a way that creates value." A sales force in Toronto sold a fleet of Mitsubishi Fuso trucks to a corporate customer. Before the contract could be inked, the customer backed out and purchased a fleet of Volvo trucks instead. How did a Volvo sales force get this customer on board? Influencing people—getting them to change their minds—is one of the toughest tasks a compliance professional could have. You can work through it by understanding the hidden powers of social psychology and the sources and drivers of influence.

The influence mosaic

Human nature is a mosaic: There are people and social elements that resist change and those that promote and support it. There always will be. Social psychologists tell us that resistance is at the heart of change, yet many of us are surprised when it emerges so suddenly that we have no opportunity to read the signs and step into a new relationship role. How do you identify and anticipate resistance? How do you harness its energy in order either to minimize it or to proceed with your agenda? Behaviorism offers us clues, and these often rely more on how you think about a particular person or situation than on the results you want and the action you take to achieve it.

People make or change decisions on the basis of whether they seek rewards ("This truck is fuel-efficient" nets a "Yes") or whether they fear punishment ("This truck may be fuel-efficient, but the price of fuel in increasing" nets a "No.") Some people are risk-takers; others, risk-avoiders. Some people do whatever they can just to maintain the balance of their status quo. Frame your initial questions of a prospect or employee with those factors in mind. Initially, you're trying to discover as much information as you can about their values, needs, and desires. Use the feedback from your questions to link your idea, program, or product to the values, needs, and desires—and yes, even fears—they're expressing. For instance, start with "what" questions: "What are you looking for in a truck?" The "what" questions can be followed by "how" questions: "How did you arrive at the decision to purchase a fleet of Mitsubishi trucks?" If you encounter resistance, pursue it with questions such as these: "Is there a reason you chose not to purchase our Mitsubishi trucks?" "Is there something specific I could do to rekindle your interest?"

Alex Lickerman, M.D., writes in *Psychology Today* that people are more likely to believe something is true if they've discovered it on their own. Rather than push your agenda to get someone to change his or her mind, frame your questions to convey how genuinely interested you are in the other person's needs, interests, and values. Lickerman suggests a face-saving way to help a person let go of an erroneous belief. "Put forth the idea that the frequency with which a person is correct and their value as a human being are two entirely separate things." A person's earlier, formative experiences may contribute to an erroneous belief or decision. Over the years, an emotional attachment will have fortified it. Take time to explore these experiences with the other person. It may give you insight into his or her reason for a particular decision and allow you to seek common ground and modify your approach. Remember, too, that people find it easier to make a decision or change their mind if they can rationally justify it. Give them a reason to do so. For example, you own a perfectly good car that's five years old but nonetheless reliable. A salesman would like you to buy a 2011 model, but you just can't justify the expense. The salesman then offers you an option: Why not lease this vehicle? It's fuel-efficient, has ample power, and even nicer—you'll have no worries over maintenance. The deal clinched!

Listening for clues

Why is it so hard to change someone's mind? Because the *real issue is changing behavior.* For example, you need to motivate employees—read that, *change their behavior*—in order to achieve 100 percent company participation in the annual Red Cross blood drive. Or perhaps a member of your sales force has to change a customer's mindset about the new features on one of your company's products. Minds don't change quickly because behavior doesn't. However, it's a safe bet to anticipate that in the future, computer-mediated technologies will hasten the ability to change minds because knowledge and input from others is a major influencer.

Howard Gardner, Harvard Business School's influential psychologist and author of several books, offers us a succinct perspective on mind-changing: "The biggest mistake people make is not understanding the other's resistances." Why? Because there's a hidden message in everything someone says—and social psychologists tell us that the speaker may not even be aware of it. This hidden "content" contains emotion, story, and possibly metaphor and simile. A speaker can be reacting to one situation, for example, while simultaneously expressing his or her beliefs about another. A speaker's "take" on a situation can be influenced by a buried storyline of earlier experiences that contains encounters with good and evil, with obstacles that couldn't be overcome, and with dictatorial, power-wielding people.

For example:

- Psychologists tell of a businesswoman who threw lavish dinner parties. The catered affairs were abundant with food, much more than was needed for the number of guests. "There's not enough food," she'd tell the caterer each time. And each time, he was able to sell her more, eventually doubling the amount of food she actually needed. (The woman's mother had abandoned her in childhood, leaving her with a profound sense of loss; she was reared in foster care, and food became her security.)

- The Midwest publisher of a monopoly city newspaper was known as an active supporter of civic events. Yet he vehemently opposed re-locating the city's annual visual and performing arts festival from a narrow, waterfront area to a more attractive, spacious area in the city's downtown civic center. He then refused to give the festival any publicity in his paper. Organizers were mystified—What was behind this obduracy?—and went ahead with the change of venue anyway, publicizing the festival instead through area weeklies, out-of-state city papers, flyers, posters, direct-mail pieces, the festival web site, and social media. They were successful, increasing festival attendance from the previous year by an additional 170,000 visitors. (A year later, they discovered the reason for the publisher's stance: He believed that prisoners housed in the nearby city jail shouldn't be allowed to look out their barred windows at the festivities, an obduracy made the more striking by discovering that he suffered from Alzheimer's disease.)

- A female dental patient was ordered to be CT-scanned for a possible bone abscess in her teeth. She refused, calling it a "poison machine." (On probing, the oral surgeon discovered that 30 years earlier, a CT scan had diagnosed the woman with a brain tumor, and she had summarily walked out of the physician's office without taking action. She was afraid now to discover that the diagnosis might be true—even though this CT scan would be of her teeth only).

Such hidden messages will influence a person's decisions and changes of mind. In most cases, you can effectively counter resistance if you will:

✓ listen for such "hidden" content and respond to it quickly by switching roles (see Chapter Three).

✓ re-frame your proposal in a positive fashion and make sure it resonates with the other person as the right message.

✓ repeat back to the other person in your own words what you believe his or her concern to be.

✓ re-focus the situation; for example, "What would happen if your company didn't replace its old fleet of trucks?"

✓ try reason and logic; that's what most business-people use in making decisions.

- ✓ ask appropriate follow-up questions.
- ✓ allow for the passage of time and unanticipated events to have hardened or softened a person's stance; e.g., the events of 9/11.
- ✓ narrate your own experiences in a similar situation (the storyline) and let the other person draw his or her own conclusions.
- ✓ make the proposal urgent.
- ✓ allow for feedback and dialogue.

Key Points in the Chapter

To change minds, you first have to change behavior, and that doesn't happen easily. You're likelier to achieve a buy or a buy-in for your proposal or decision if you understand the inner dynamics of influence. People are likelier to accept new information, say social psychologists, if it reinforces their beliefs. If it doesn't, resistance kicks in, and resistance is at the heart of change. To counter this, find out as much information as you can about the values, needs, desires, and even fears, of your prospect. Use the feedback from these questions to reframe your suggestions and link them to your selling points. Provide your prospect with justification for agreeing with you. Then look for the hidden messages in a prospect's response. By listening for the hidden content, you can respond by quickly switching roles, re-focusing the situation, asking follow-up questions, repeating back in your own words what you believe the prospect's concerns to be, and using various appeals to reason and logic.

CHAPTER TWO

THE POWER OF INFLUENCE

You can impact behavior by harnessing your objectives to the five powerful sources of Influence:

- Peer pressure—"Other people believe this, therefore I should, too" is a powerful social force in getting compliance to change behavior. Remember the strength found in numbers: If a number of people evidence the desired behavior change, make sure to harness the influence of social networks, both viral and online as may be appropriate.

- Rewards and Incentives—These aren't the same thing. One is thanks, the other is encouragement. *Rewards* are tied to the outcome; for example, recognition for a job done well or an acknowledgment for having made the correct decision. *Incentives*, however, are the things one knows about beforehand. They speak to compensation, financial or otherwise; for example, an account executive for a dental supply firm knows in advance that she'll receive a bonus if she exceeds her monthly sales quota. Make sure to tie rewards to the actual behavior in a situation—e.g., to the *correctness* of purchasing Volvo trucks—and not to the outcome—to the actual purchase of them. Ultimately, your purpose in changing behavior is to change the mindset behind it.

When a business goes through organizational change, the work situation can reach critical proportion. Employees are likely to fear and resist the changes. Morale may become low, productivity may decrease. You need to leverage your influence, but you see it being chipped away by a vocal minority of disaffected employees who already hold some social influence in the organization. They, in turn, are influencing others. How did that come about? Early researchers such as Hickson, Hinings, Lee and Schneck discovered in 1971 that anyone in an organization or any part of it with control over resources creates what is called a "resource dependency." This automatically gives them power over others. Can you reverse it? No. Can you moderate it? Yes. Try smoothing the transition for everyone by implementing a system of rewards and incentives compatible with the strategies of change. Put some creative thought into it: You need to design incentives that will change people's minds about the new values and desired behaviors.

- Social motivation—The potential in sheer numbers of people isn't enough. You want *active influencers*—the motivators who are willing to share their experiences and offer support, information, and referrals to others. While numbers are attractive in determining market share—the connecting power of Facebook and Twitter nicely provide this—the plain fact is that a much smaller number of people are the real influencers in any business situation. Find those influencers and rely on them to reinforce changes in thought and behavior.

- Environment—You can control the environment to produce the desired change. Where you choose to conduct business—one on one in your office or in a prospect's place of business, in an employee's work zone, in a neutral place—will influence the outcome of any negotiation. Make sure the environment you choose offers positive reinforcement by providing actual examples of the desired mind-change at work—mirroring it. If negotiating with all your employees for a desired change of behavior, you may have to "enable" the decision you want by offering a reward—for example, a permanent modification in the physical work environment to make it less stressful for employees.

- Reinforcement—A behavior change requires repetition and positive reinforcement. A speech to employees, for example, can be reinforced with personal e-mail messages and by group leaders in meeting. Visual images such as those on posters or in a Power Point presentation can also reinforce the desired change; so can reframing the original message. Beware of relying on gifts or other tangible rewards; they'll reinforce the message initially, but once gone, so is the new behavior.

Avoiding confusion

Is influence the same as power? As authority? As leadership? History places the mantle of greatness on leaders: Hannibal, Napolean, Churchill, Eisenhower, Lincoln, Roosevelt—all larger than life, an historical perspective fueled by historians and stoked by the mass media. It's a myth. At least in the 21st Century, people regard good leaders as collaborators. These are the people who exert influence in a way that emphasizes relationships and a cooperative approach to problem solving. In other words, authority, leadership, power—these can't be exercised at all unless relationships first activate them. You may have authority to make decisions and command others in the workforce—but that doesn't make you influential or a good leader. Does power? Researchers have disagreed about that for decades. Some describe leadership as a power relationship. Others say "power" and "influence" are the same thing. Researcher and author Joseph Rost reports that "leadership is an influence relationship among leaders and followers who intend real changes that reflect their mutual purposes." Confusing, isn't it? Your best bet? Since 21st Century leadership is collaborative, think of leadership as the hub of a wheel with each person in the relationship one of the spokes. Since a wheel can't function as a wheel without its spokes, each person, or spoke, has a certain degree of influence that impacts a project, decision, or proposal. Doesn't this sound like an easy and equitable way to conduct business? In an imaginary world—perhaps a world of the future—it would be. The wheel would go 'round and around, its "spokes" peacefully executing projects and solving problems. However, people have their own agendas—some of it hidden even to them—and this reduces the likelihood of your getting mostly "yes" to any proposal.

The give and take of influence

Influence, however, is multi-faceted and can be viewed in various ways. For instance, have you ever bought a drink for a business acquaintance or invested in the stock market? The oldest method of market exchange known even to prehistoric man, the reciprocity of "I-give-to-you, you-give-to-me-in-return" is an accepted survival technique that promises returns in one of three ways: a return of equal value in a specified time, a "trust" return assumed to balance out to equal value with type and time of return unspecified, and what is called "negative" reciprocity: The giver gets nothing for having given up or sacrificed. Most of us are familiar with the reciprocity of the West Coast potlatch. In the potlatch, First Nation peoples demonstrate their wealth and status by giving away precious possessions as gifts, thus prompting recipients to reciprocate in kind at some future point.

The reciprocity of influence implies not only a bargain but an obligation: What I provide you, you agree to repay me. This allows me to make plans for the organization and to establish a relationship with you that may reward us both in the future. In a sense, your obligation now binds you to me. Numerous such obligations for co-operative gains will create a network of others that we call community. But reciprocal giving can be manipulative, and I advise you to use influence ethically. For example, what about giving something to someone *before* requesting a return (the proverbial business drink)? The "law" of reciprocity says, "do it" because the implied obligation is a powerful tactic to gain compliance. Yet if it's you who accepted the favor or gift, aren't you likely to feel uncomfortable until you return the favor—and as a result, don't you often agree to a favor requested of you that's larger than the one you originally accepted? And isn't there something in human nature that makes us continue to grant these requests and give concessions? You can turn down the initial favor or gift, of course. But to avoid being manipulated if you've accepted it, make sure your eyes are wide open: It may be a manipulative gesture, and you're not obligated to return that.

Are you consistent?

Does what you say reflect your beliefs? Do you take action on the basis of those beliefs? Hefty lawsuits against U.S. tobacco manufacturers show that people often violate what they personally hold to be true. And that once having made a decision, there's a strong, internal drive to be consistent with it. That's how we justify our original decision: We make future decisions based on it. Yet consistency is an automatic response, a motive for taking action that's a reputation-builder valued like money in the bank. After all, you don't want to be seen as weak and inconsistent. Consistency makes our lives orderly. We need only believe, say, or do whatever is consistent with our earlier decision. Unfortunately, this shortcut is also a mindless response, one that can hide our inner fears and true beliefs. What triggers consistency? Social psychologists say that it's commitment. For example, 10 years ago I thought you needed a new fleet of trucks for your business, and I approached you with a good offer. You made a commitment to buy and signed the contract. Now, with gas prices skyrocketing, my company has come out with a fuel-efficient line of trucks so competitive with others in their class that people are taking notice. I approach you again with a new offer. Not wanting to appear inconsistent with your earlier commitment to me, you sign the new contract.

Find like-minded people

Has your truck customer made the right decision? Did he really sign the contract to be consistent with his earlier commitment? Or did he also ink the contract on the basis of what he saw and knew other customers were doing? Could he have made a better deal elsewhere? Social proof will influence decisions when a customer—or even an employee—is uncertain about taking the action requested. In this scenario, you'll achieve buy-in when the targeted individual sees other people taking the same action. In the second scenario, you can expect that an individual will buy into a request if he or she sees similar, like-minded people acting in situations similar to what you proposed.

Do we fit?

People more readily accept decisions from those they know and like. In fact, marketing analysts reveal that the "I like you/I know you" social bond has more influence on a purchase decision or buy-in than the attributes of a product, service, or decision itself. A negotiation slathered in flattery may charm a snake for a short fix, but it won't produce long-term, repeat results. Here's the corollary to this: People tend to buy from others who resemble them in physical appearance, dress, gender, background, activities, education, and culture. If you don't fit the bill with personal history and homogeneity, what can you do? Start today to build rapport with your people, contacts, and customers. Build a foundation you can stand on in the future by being genuinely interested in their welfare. Put people at ease with you. Ask about their family, chat about business, find things to talk about that you both share. Step into a long-lasting relationship role with them that fits (see Chapter Three). Remember, too, that people who interact only with those they know and like usually fail to recognize the merits of otherwise good offers and decisions that could advance their goals.

Mark Anthony, a friend and supporter of Julius Caesar, built instant rapport with the skeptical people of ancient Rome by eulogizing Caesar on his death with an adroit public speech that identified his interests with theirs:

> "Friends, Romans, Countrymen, lend me your ears. I have come to bury Caesar, not to praise him. The evil that men do lives after them; the good is oft interred with their bones. So let it be with Caesar. The noble Brutus hath told you Caesar was ambitious: If it were so, it was a grievous fault, and grievously hath

> Caesar answered it. Here, under leave of Brutus and the rest, (for Brutus is an honorable man; so are they all, all honorable men) come I to speak in Caesar's funeral. He was my friend, faithful and just to me. But Brutus says he was ambitious, and Brutus is an honorable man. He hath brought many captives home to Rome, whose ransoms did the general coffers fill. Did this in Caesar seem ambitious? When that the poor hath cried, Caesar hath wept. Ambition should be made of sterner stuff: Yet Brutus says he was ambitious, And Brutus is an honorable man…."

Do we complement each other?

Personality is factored into any influence situation. Just as people are more comfortable buying from those they know and like who are similar to them, they'll find you, your products, or your suggestions more desirable if your attitude is positive, your personality forceful and likeable, and you demonstrate both competence and integrity. People also like others who complement them.

Act now!

"Act now! Only five days left!" "Lost our lease! Closing our doors for good!" "Space is limited! Reserve your spot now!" "All summer merchandise 30% off! Sale ends Saturday!" The "don't-leave-home-without-it" sell lines show how scarcity can work in your favor. People jump at these chances. They hurry to buy some item that's limited by time and number and soon won't be accessible to them. They buy into some decision or opportunity that soon will disappear ("Act now!"), is offered exclusively to only a few ("Be the first to drive a new Fu Dawei!"), and to the fear or being left out ("Don't be the last to know!"). Why? Because the prospect of taking a loss or being denied something becomes value-enhanced whether it's worth it or not.

"Don't leave home without it" works successfully when two conditions are present. An item can't simply *be* scarce; it has to be *newly* scarce. And it has to operate in a competitive situation with buyers scrambling to be first, fighting over a scarce item, or besting each other in the auction barn, for example. What are the implications for you? Ethically, you want your proposal, your decision, your product, to be evaluated on its long-term merits. Yet we all know that buyers in a "Sale-Ends-Saturday" situation run more on emotion than logic. You can capitalize on this for periodic short-term gains, particularly in sales and with teams in the workplace. But for long-term gains—and solid relationships—you're better off offering incentives than using sometimes duplicitous tactics.

Salute the symbol.

It's human nature. When anyone in an authority position—father, boss, teacher—tells us to do something, we usually find ways to comply. By complying, we demonstrate the conduct thought to be correct for the situation. However, this, too, is an automatic response. We're reacting to the symbols of authority, not to the actual person. An Army private salutes the uniform, not the individual wearing it. In business, in any social situation, authority can have its pros and cons. We naturally expect the person in authority to have the knowledge, the influence, the morals, the respect to command leadership. But we chafe because experience has shown us that this is not always the case. Study what happened at Enron. Not all people in authority are trustworthy. Not all are honest. Many don't have our best interests at heart. And often, we find out too late.

New challenges

How we work, where we work are far cries from earlier generations. Driven by technology and global forces, changes have forged new work environments and a new style of working. As organizations respond to the demands of worldwide competition and diminishing budgets, we're all being pushed to work harder and smarter. Collaboration rewards us with those smart outcomes. But collaboration means teamwork and teamwork demands mutual dependence. Frankly, today's Knowledge Age doesn't give us opportunity to build relationships slowly and carefully, allowing us to build trust over time. The web of interactions that comes from working closely with others and depending on them to do their part have become complex; at times, they may even seem overwhelming. This type of environment is advantageous for developing your influence skills. Just make sure not to lose sight of your personal goals and not to get mired in a situation that isn't of your making.

Different situations will call on you to assume different roles. Assuming those relationship roles will be easier if you routinely are supportive of co-workers, help others to succeed, and give credit when credit is due. But murky relationships—a past history of differences with another person—can interfere with positive influence, making it hard to determine your influence objective and stick to it. For instance, how do you put aside personal differences with a co-worker or co-leader to become an ally when a situation demands it? How do you assume the role of *Friend* to someone you never liked? Admittedly, it's difficult. However, influence will tell you to keep your focus on the new roles you're being asked to assume and to view resolution of the current situation as a joint effort, a cooperative, collaborative one that in process should heal past differences. Remember that the appropriate use of influence will add value to your relationships. And that the people you think of as "just naturally influential," usually are not. They have worked for years at developing mutually beneficial relationships. They have invested time—sometimes even money—to learn the skills necessary for building a sphere of influence. And they wield that influence positively, honestly, and with trust.

Key Points in the Chapter

People cling strongly to their values. If changes at work appear to contradict them, you can moderate resistance by implementing a system of rewards and incentives to change people's minds about the new values and desired behaviors. Remember that peer pressure strongly influences mindsets. Tapping into social networks both viral and online can help mitigate resistance, but only if you find the active influencers in the networks and rely on them to reinforce the changes desired. Message reinforcement also benefits from your choice of physical environments and media. You can influence behavior in a variety of ways—by acting on what you believe, by understanding the unspoken "contracts" of bargains and obligations, by establishing rapport and investing time and attention in others, by exhibiting a positive personality, and by choosing incentives over "don't-leave-home-without-it" tactics.

The next few pages are blank. Take a few minutes to jot down your reflections about some past situations you wish you had handled better and to briefly describe a few that you currently face. Then read on to discover in the following chapters how role sequencing can help you establish and keep influence.

I wish I had____________________________________

(2)____

(3)____

Right now, I'm being asked to____________________

(2)____

(3)____

Other Notes

CHAPTER THREE

THE IMPORTANCE OF ROLES AND CUES

In today's fast-paced, highly competitive market for goods and services, the pressure to produce results has never been greater. The relationships you carve now are vital to getting work done and done right. For instance, you've scheduled an appointment with a prospect for later today. You've sharpened your proposal, believe your timing is appropriate, and decided that it will be an easy "sell." To your dismay, the prospect is impressed with the proposal but decides not to act on it at this time. What can you do? What should you have done? Actively pitch it? Remind her what the competition is doing and that her company will lose out if she doesn't act now? Do a little underhanded manipulation? Cozy up to her as a (false) friend?

Whoa! Don't conduct business blindly. Like a performer taking his cues from the director in the control booth, the part you play in any relationship should be based partly on the cues you receive from the other person. You can take the anxiety out of any negotiation and parlay those cues into success by stepping into one of five roles—and letting the cues dictate the one you should start with and those to which you should progress. For example, your goal may be pitchman. But if you assume that role at the start of negotiations and persist in it when a cue tells you otherwise, you risk business failure. To get to that point, you may first have to assume another role, perhaps two. The five roles below are part of an interpersonal skills system of influence that is at once comprehensive, intuitive, and powerful:

- *Change Agent*
- *Consultant*
- *Pitchman/Pitchwoman*
- *Ally*
- *Friend*

The next chapters provide in-depth information on each role. For now, here's a look at some fairly typical scenarios that will cue you to the proper role:

Your boss was persuaded by the corporate marketing director that sponsoring a community-wide art festival for schoolchildren on the grounds would burnish the corporate reputation as a good neighbor/good citizen. In the long run, it would be good for business. However, he balked at the suggestion that the winning pieces be hung and displayed inside corporate headquarters for everyone to file in and view. The role cued you? *Change Agent.*

The university has just hired an older woman to handle the school's semester-abroad program. While the new hire speaks several languages and is an experienced faculty member and foreign traveler, she has no experience with government regulations, requirements, and restrictions on foreign travel. As the vice-president of human relations, you keep your eye on things and can see that the woman is visibly upset. Finally she approaches you, confessing her inexperience. "I want to help the students," she says, "but obviously I need training. What should I do?" The role just cued you? *Consultant.*

Your firm sells industrial cleaners to customers in a 10-county area. As the head of sales, you notice there are a number of potential customers in an untapped county that caters to tourism; that county, you believe, should sell well. Your boss isn't convinced. "Given the price of gas for our trucks," he says, "it's just not cost-effective to service that county: It's too far away." You set out to convince him otherwise. Your role here: *Pitchman/ Pitchwoman.*

A 501C(3) not-for-profit had a difficult time signing up potential donors for bone marrow cells, blood stem cells, and cord blood among members of the African American communities in the state. The CEO of the organization, a Caucasian, sought outside counsel who advised her to hire an experienced African American woman with contacts in these communities to head up her annual, statewide donor drive. The role for her new hire? *Ally.*

The ADON in your health center has just volunteered to take on new responsibilities in addition to her current ones. As marketing director, you know that her new duties devolved from the new objectives you developed for the health center. You and she have worked closely together on projects in the past, and as you hear her sigh, you know she feels overworked. Over lunch, you commiserate with her and ask how you can help. Your role here? *Friend.*

The cues

Not all cues are vocal, and you need to be mindful of them all in switching roles. Some of them are spatial—a chair that was next to a desk has now been placed across from the desk, a client or customer stands farther away from you (or closer to you) than you're comfortable with; some are physical—a female co-worker places a reassuring hand on your arm or a male colleague slaps you heartily on the back, a team member in one-on-one has crossed his legs away from you and assumed a sideways profile; some are vocal but not verbalized—a sigh, a grunt, a nervous cough in the auditorium—all cues. Be mindful also that in any dialogue or negotiation you, yourself, are giving out nonverbal and vocal cues. Since most of us remain mindful of the words we say, nonverbal information is the tattletale, communicating approximately two-thirds of the information, according to Ray Birdwhistle, premier researcher on nonverbal communication. The remaining information comes from our words and how we speak them—tone, pitch, rate, speed, volume.

Voice and personality researchers J. Clarke Weaver and Nancy M. Hamilton caution that your tone, pitch, and volume may give off the wrong cues. For instance, you intend the conversation with a customer to be friendly, but your voice is thin, and your pitch and tone are off-putting. The pair suggests you remedy this by a series of preparatory deep-breathing exercises from the diaphragm. And in today's high-pitched society, where voices are taut with impatience, sharp with nasality from failing to breathe properly, and one high pitch tends to mirror another's, women even more than men risk giving off the wrong cues. By failing to pitch their voices to the mid-range used by such TV personalities as Oprah Winfrey, Diane Sawyer, and Anne Curry, women lose credibility. Men, too, become more credible if the voice is pitched mid-range or lower. Vocal cues speak volumes: They can indicate agreement (a murmur of assent), boredom or doubt (throat-clearing), or disagreement (hissing).

Verbal cues such as the following tend to sink a negotiation. They're time-wasters, imprecise, and in some cases ungrammatical:

- "It's like, well, you know." Or, "Like, I think I'll order the peas."
- "Awesome"
- "Amazing"
- "Dude"
- "I and Jim" or, "Me and Jim."

The words you chose can miscue the listener in other ways. For instance, the word "economizing" in a sales pitch may mean one thing to you, another to your customer. A bare-bones message from the team leader may lack enough detail for team members to act on it. A lack of shared meaning between you and your Cambodian counterpart fails to produce positive results; in other words, you can't sell snow to an Amazonian whose language doesn't contain a word for it.

A photographer friend of mine was on assignment in Germany to photograph students at the woodcarving school in Oberammergau. He worked quietly and patiently, not cuing the students, simply lining up good shots of carving as they occurred. But to his dismay, every time he lined up a good composition, the student would shift his hands and, it seemed, deliberately turn aside. On his first foray to Germany, my frustrated photographer friend learned a valuable lesson from this encounter: Spatial relationships differ from culture to culture, and by standing close to the students to capture hands at work, he had encroached on intimate distance. Later that week, my friend learned another lesson when a

German photojournalist invited him to lunch at a Munich restaurant renowned for its sauerbraten. Accustomed to lightweight North American restaurant tables and a convivial atmosphere among patrons, my friend discovered instead that square tables and chairs, too heavy to move easily for conviviality and spaced widely apart in the restaurant, discouraged close-up conversations and the friendly give-and-take of noise among tables.

Edward T. Hall, the benchmark researcher on proxemics, the science of spatial relationships, provides us valuable information on nonverbal cue strategy. Hall subdivides space into four dimensions, starting from the widest, or public dimension, through the dimension allocated to social or consultative discourse, followed by casual, or personal space, to the closest dimension, the one reserved for intimacy. The dimensions for each category differ from culture to culture. A meeting between a Chinese national and a Canadian national, for example, has to be carefully arranged for fear of offending: While the social or consultative distance for a North American (Hall says 4 to 12 feet) is actually *wider* than that proscribed by Chinese culture for conversations between two people well-acquainted, formality requires the North American keep a *greater* distance between the two. Compare this with a conversation between two businessmen from Yemen. The social-consultative distance now *narrows* because traditional Arab culture requires a person stand close in order to gauge the other's temperament.

Your posture, your dress, your body language—these physical expressions of *you* cue volumes about your intent and emotional state. In conversation, do you look directly at the other person—does the other person in negotiation look directly at you? An indirect or shifting gaze can cue caution, lack of trust, uncertainty, insecurity, even insincerity. In another culture, however, a direct look at someone will be misinterpreted. Do you try to gain control of a business situation by touching, placing your hand on someone's arm; in other words, trying to be a friend? When in meeting, do you listen with legs crossed *away* from the speaker (avoidance, lack of receptivity)? In negotiations, do you tend to keep your hands in your pockets or folded (closed, unreceptive, suspicious)? While a neat and attractive physical appearance can gain your points, do you tend to dress *better* than your customer, client, or boss (competitiveness, superiority)? Do you groom your face and hair during negotiations (more interested in yourself than your counterpart)? Do you constantly throw your hair back or wear it long over your eyes (deceit, conceit)? Do your verbal and nonverbal behaviors agree with each other? Perhaps not; for example, you may be smiling at something a colleague says (because it's politic to do so), but your posture indicates avoidance or antagonism: The two should be congruent. And have you read correctly that a colleague leaning forward in the chair is interested in what you're saying?

Introducing those negative, self-talk gremlins

Before assuming a role or transitioning from one to another, you'll need to re-program your self-talk gremlins. Those nasty little voices inside your head—some of them conscious, some of them unconscious—are ready to derail you from marshaling the confidence and focus you need to face any challenge and take positive action. You've heard those voices before; their job is to scare you and stop you, and keep you right where you are. They sound like this:

- "I've never been any good at this, so why try?"
- "I can't do it."
- "It happened to me five years ago, and here it is happening again."
- "I always fail at things like this."
- "They should choose someone else."

Really? You can't be that bad—can you? Of course not. Just like everyone else, you've had some bad experiences in life, some missteps and failures. You moved on, of course, but like most of us, you not only picked yourself up but packed up a suitcase of those failures and mistakes and brought it along with you into the present. These are your gremlins. Whispering in your ear, they tell you how to perceive and interpret every situation. They lurk behind every challenge you face, every thought you have. They fight hard to maintain the status quo, depriving you of self-confidence and energy, undercutting your abilities and your chances for success, lurking behind every challenge you face.

You can overcome the negative self-talk. Psychologists tell us that self-talk carves neural pathways in the brain that later program our thinking and behavior. If your self-talk tends to be positive, it will strengthen those positive pathways; if it is constantly negative and fearful, the pathways will be similarly reinforced. *Speak back to those negative self-talk gremlins.* By using identity meditations, or positive self-talk, you can reprogram your habits of thinking and behaving and etch new neural pathways. Over time, the new habits will be strengthened, overpowering and rendering harmless the old, neural pathways of negativity and self-doubt.

Identity meditations

You can move into a new role or transition from one to another through identity meditation. What do you say to yourself to get the confidence and focus to take positive action? There are no *right* words, only *your* words, and you already use them every day to initiate or carry through on a challenging activity, block out stressors, and overcome negative self-talk. Use these identity meditations now. You need only a word, perhaps a phrase, which silently affirms confidence in your ability to take on the challenge of a new role. You can do it.

Key Points in the Chapter

Before assuming a role or transitioning from one to another, strategically use and constantly monitor the verbal, vocal, and nonverbal cues that can help guarantee success in any business situation. Consider these cues foreplay to the roles you'll assume in negotiations. (See the following chapters for an explanation of the roles.) Among the several categories of clues, the nonverbal dimension is the most telling, accounting for nearly two-thirds of the information transmitted in meetings or conversations. Since the width, as measured by inches and feet, of spatial relationships differ from culture to culture and the nature of discourse, it is wise to plan meetings and conversations carefully and to be just as careful in monitoring the clues you transmit and those you receive. Make sure to re-program the self-talk gremlins when faced with a new role. Your inner voices that speak of doubts and failures can keep you from succeeding in any role you assume. Use a word, a phrase, perhaps a sentence of identity meditation to affirm self-confidence in your ability.

CHAPTER FOUR

CHANGE AGENT

When a process for change and direct coaching are required to move your partner forward in a positive direction.

You were brought into the marketing department of a major hotel chain with a mandate to streamline operations. For starters, it's certain you're going to have to fire some people. You spend 30 days working with the staff. They're all good people. Each has something to contribute to the marketing effort. Mary's fairly new, but she's motivated. Bill has a wife and three little children; he thinks of others. Frank is an older guy, seasoned by 20 years in the business, 17 of them with the company. The public relations manager has been using social media efficiently to create renewed public awareness of the brand. Advertising hopes to create a new campaign to spark business. In fact, each member of the marketing team has something worthwhile to contribute. You could streamline operations by consolidating some of the functions under fewer titles, of course. But actually fire people? What would that do to morale? Won't the remaining staffers complain about the additional responsibilities? Suppose they rebel? Won't that create more headaches for you than not? You spend sleepless nights worrying. You're no Donald Trump, after all. How should you approach this? You meet Monday with Frank, the seasoned staffer. He seems nervous and even stumbles over his words. "I'm stuck," he finally admits. "I've been working here all these years, and it seems like I'm getting nowhere." Frank has just cued you to *Change Agent*. That starts a new thought process. Could the department actually become *more* efficient and productive without having to fire several members?

The next scenario is less obvious. For several years, three faculty members on the 18-person teaching staff in a university anthropology department have been undercutting Sheila's efforts to improve the urban anthropology sequence. For the last 8 semesters, Sheila had been taking students on field trips to gain practical experience. On Friday, Sheila was shocked to learn that a faculty member had brought one of her male students to tears in class by his snide remarks about an upcoming field trip she had planned. Sheila was livid.

You have known Sheila for years and know she is struggling. She says to you: "I've been with the university several years. Here I am trying to accomplish something good for the students, but no one on the faculty seems to want it. They don't want me here, that's obvious." I'm resigning at the end of the semester." In this scenario—a true one, by the way—Sheila has just offered you a cue to the *Change Agent* role. We define it as *when a process for change and direct coaching are required to move your partner forward in a positive direction.*

Moving your partner forward in a positive direction, however, carries risks. Are you manipulating her? Examine your motivation, your objective. Are you wearing the dark hat, or the white one? As an influence agent, you want to help people improve and to add meaning to their lives. As a manipulator, you're subtly devious, tricking others into doing your bidding. Even though it may be unintentional, you're trafficking in influence on the dark side. Stand back for a moment. Are you being self-serving? Or are you treating people with honesty and the respect they deserve?

Identity meditation for the role of Change Agent

How do you get ready to support an individual especially if your own self-talk gremlin is whispering in your ear? It's time to use identity meditation by drawing on your positive inner voices. An identity meditation should be practiced before initiating any new role or facing any new or challenging activity. For the above scenario: *"I see the value in these field trips, so do most of the faculty members, and so do the department chair and the dean, who support Sheila. I will further support her to make the best decision for her career. I will be her change agent."* Meditating on the positive assets without distraction will allow you to align with your deepest values and to focus on the *essence* of your thoughts. Now you're able to draw on your positive emotions and capabilities and can repeatedly reaffirm them.

The identity meditation has helped you assume the role as *Change Agent*. You've been prompted to help Sheila re-examine the realities of the faculty situation and her own perspective. You help her realize she has other options and move her in a positive direction. You also help her re-program her self-talk gremlin, and move forward with a level head.

Is the role of Change Agent first?

While you now have identified the end role needed, be aware that you may first have to assume one or more of the other roles listed earlier—*Ally* (Chapter 7) or *Friend* (Chapter 8), for example—before assuming the role of *Change Agent*. Handled successfully, a *Change Agent* can make what is apparently undesirable more desirable to all concerned without rancor or fanfare. Make sure to first assess just how ready for change an individual, team, department, or project manager is. These four states of readiness for change will clue you to your first role:

- Precontemplation: The person is unaware of the need to change.

- Contemplation: The person is thinking about change.

- Preparation: The person has already thought about the situation and is moving in the direction of taking action.

- Action: The person is in full action mode.

Remember that when action has begun, it will be necessary to maintain the change.

Change Agent contexts

Among the several contexts where a *Change Agent* is dictated, three stand out:

- Time constraints dictate joint action; you won't have the luxury of simply sitting and reflecting on the need for change, or the time to over-analyze the situation.

- The other person may use such clue words as being "stymied," frozen," or "stuck."

- Change will be trickier than meets the eye due to obstacles in work and life.

Let's see how this can play out. An acquaintance is an account executive in the branch office of a major public relations agency. Her new boss, she said, is a workaholic. A few months ago, he opened the branch office in question to meet the needs of a Fortune 50 industrial client who wants him to be a hand-holder. Your friend's boss wants her to be one, too, not only requiring that she be available 24/7 but that she dines with the client liaison, party with him, and stay up until all hours if client just wants to talk or drink. Your friend says this is unacceptable and unprofessional behavior. Although she needs the job, she's stymied and plans to quit at week's end. As her friend and chair of the local chapter of the Public Relations Society of America, you want to help her. You don't have much time. The word "stymied" has cued you to *Change Agent*. But change will be tricky in this case, and you'll have to choose one or more alternate roles first.

Smart goals

As an *appointed*, rather than opportunistic, *Change Agent*—the hotel chain scenario—you'll be expected to demonstrate certain behaviors and core competencies. Primary among these is the wisdom and patience to craft on paper certain S.M.A.R.T. project or assignment goals.

S. The goals must be <u>specific</u>. What is it, who is involved, when is the start date and the deadline for completion, why do it at all (specific reasons), where is it to occur, what are the constraints, requirements, and limitations?

M. The tasks that lead up to the final project and the final project itself must be <u>measurable</u>. Establish the units of measurement beforehand. How will you evaluate it? Which criteria will be used to evaluate it? Which mid-point evaluative criteria will allow you to make course corrections if not on target?

A. Project goals must be attainable. If a goal begs to be completed, even if self-determined, you should craft a plan to develop the attitudes, skill and abilities, opportunities, tools, support, and knowledge to bring that goal to fruition. By listing your goals on paper, you're developing a mental image of success that will bring you closer to goal attainment.

R. Seven-league boots went out with Puss and the fairy tale. Goals must be realistic. Whether you set your goal high or low, you still have to be able to accomplish it step by step.

T. A goal needs a timeframe. By giving it a timeframe, you'll establish the urgency you need to succeed.

Goal achievement also benefits from milestones. These serve as mid-point markers and motivators to keep you going. Make sure to keep the goal in plain sight by jointly setting certain milestones with the other person or with your team. Your final task is of utmost importance: Create a vision of the future with your partner or team. The vision is a success story that is described in vivid detail. It should embody everything that you and your partner or team are working toward, and everyone needs to embrace it.

Key Points in the Chapter

Some people are natural change agents and slip into that role effortlessly. For others, systematically pursuing the tactics described in this chapter will produce success. Chief among them is the re-programming of self-talk gremlins, those little voices in the head that can derail success. Approach any possible situation calling for a *Change Agent* by first using an identity meditation to get you into the role. You may have to assume one or more intermediate roles before your end role as *Change Agent*. Draw up a S.M.A.R.T. list of goals to chart your course. Those goals have to be specific, measurable, attainable, and accomplishable within a set timeframe. Make sure also to jointly set milestones along the way and to create a vision of the completed project that all can share.

CHAPTER FIVE

CONSULTANT

To add value beyond expectations through intellectual capital.

Frank, a photographer acquaintance of yours who made his reputation in the '80s with outstanding photographs of medical breakthroughs has just been told by the Chicago agency which reps him that he must switch to digital. Although you're an amateur photographer, Frank knows you're expert in digital equipment. "What can I do?" he asks you nervously. "I don't know digital at all, and I don't have much money to invest in new equipment. Can you help me?"

The bookkeeper for a small business is in her middle years. Her computer knowledge and experience is limited, and she regards the computer sitting on her desk as an enemy to be avoided. She keeps the books by hand, and her databases, bills, receipts, and invoices are kept in individual file folders. The boss, however, knows that the business could be run more efficiently. He hires you as outside consultant to install software on her computer and spend a week tutoring her and fine-tuning the record-keeping operation. The bookkeeper resists, saying she's "too old to learn new tricks."

Jill, a recent college graduate, is a new hire in a public opinion research organization. One of her responsibilities is to run focus groups on new products. Just the other day, you saw her leafing furtively through several hardbound books on gauging public opinion and believe that she's uncertain how to proceed. Do you tell the head of the company? Or do you respond to Jill's pretty obvious need for assistance?

Becoming a professional consultant takes years of training. However, many people already possess the skill set even if they aren't aware of it. The purpose is to mentor. Whether opportunistic or intentional, in the consultant role, you'll function in one, perhaps all, of three contexts:

- A lack of knowledge, skill, wisdom, or insight—call it intellectual capital—are keeping the other person from his or her vital goals.
- The other person has taken some action, but at the expense of first analyzing the situation in order to make an effective decision.
- The other person seems blurry about what he or she needs to know and how to get that knowledge.

This is where you come in. You're in place to help the other person look at his or her concerns objectively and to clarify them. Use questions such as these to help the client:

- What piece of intellectual capital, or information, is missing for you?
- What are your goals? How can they benefit from resolving the current situation?
- What is there in your background and experience that's relevant to the situation?

Self-talk gremlins and the identity meditation

You've been cued to the role of *Consultant* in several ways. Perhaps you heard the word "help" or "I'm at a loss here. What do I do?" On the other hand, you deliberately may have been hired as a consultant or, in addition to your other responsibilities, assigned it. In any event, I caution you to watch out for negative self-talk, those gremlins in your head that you need to re-program when faced with a difficult task or a difficult person. When you hear statements from the client or other person such as, "I can't do it" or "What can I do?" or "I'm too old to learn new tricks," you realize that immediately assuming the role of *Change Agent* would cast you into a brick wall: Your frustrated client, co-worker, or friend is aware that the situation is muddled but remains unaware of the need to change and be coached. This first state of readiness—pre-contemplation—clues you to assume the role of *Consultant*.

To successfully act as *Consultant*, make sure to re-program your self-talk gremlins before tackling whatever gremlins may handicap your client. If your inner voices say "I always fail when dealing with people who are like this" or "They really should choose someone else to handle this," or "I don't know enough to do this," you know at once that you have to speak back to the self-talk gremlins to give you the confidence and inspiration to follow through with this challenging task. Which identity meditation should you use to take positive action? This is your choice. Remember that there are no *right* words, only *your* words, and you already use them every day to initiate or carry through on a challenging activity. A word, a phrase—that's all you need to silently affirm confidence in your ability to handle this situation and counsel the client or other person.

Now study the realities of the situation from your client's perspective. He or she knew some time ago that film photography is mostly outmoded, that the contemporary business world files data and keeps records efficiently via computer software, and that most marketing analysis today requires the use of focus groups. What has been stopping your client from gathering the information needed to make the necessary change? Money? Lack of encouragement? Fear of change or of trying new things? Fear of taking a risk? Fear of failure? You find that the most logical answer lies in the safety of status quoism. Your client is afraid to try something new, afraid to take what he or she perceives as a risk; in other words, your client is afraid of failing. The self-talk gremlin sounds like this: "I'm okay with doing things the way I am now. What if I fail when I try something new? I could be fired." These self-talk gremlins handicap the situation. How can you help someone start to change a negative perception (the nasty self-talk gremlin)? Be a *Change Agent* first. In the situations above, ask your client a series of *Change Agent* questions such as these to begin to move him in a positive direction:

- "How long have you been a successful photographer (or bookkeeper)?
- Do you enjoy the work?
- Do people sometimes ask you for advice about a particular photograph or photographic technique (a bookkeeping record or bookkeeping technique)? Are you able to help them?

For the recent college graduate and new hire in the public opinion research firm, try questions such as these:

- Do you like the field of public opinion research?
- How did you become interested in it?
- Much of what happens in the business world today deals with public opinion: Do you find that

other people don't understand it? Do they ask you to explain it?

Responses to questions such as these are affirming, leading clients to re-discover their skills and potentials on their own and in process, to craft identity meditations that work.

Choose your behaviors wisely.

Keep in mind that as a *Consultant*, you're in place to deliver on a need. The behaviors you choose for this can range from analyzing a situation creatively, to delivering information that's grounded in research and fact-finding, to clarifying missing principles for your client or other person. How would you creatively analyze a particular situation? Try conducting a formalized analysis to strengthen and simplify decision-making. For instance:

- Conduct a SWOT analysis (Strengths, Weaknesses, Opportunities, and Threats) to help you plan and focus on key issues. Help the other person or client to examine his or her strengths and weaknesses (the internal factors), then examine the external environment for opportunities and threats that can help or hinder achievement.

- With the client, playfully break up the problem into pieces. This helps you discard what isn't relevant to the situation (distractions), reassemble it, and examine it.

What about using research and fact-finding to deliver unexpected results for your client? Chosen wisely for its high-value content, new information can carry an element of surprise and even exceed client's expectations. Make sure, however, to avoid information overload. Instead, choose only those pieces of information that speak directly to client's need. You may want to search other disciplines for what you need, too. For example, you know that your bookkeeping client is unlikely to check online sources for help when you leave. You also know that while she's a magazine reader, her choices run to *MORE* and *AARP The Magazine*, both of them focused on mature readers. However, you've researched the magazine market and discovered that other bookkeepers need computer help, too, and they get it through the question-and-answer section of *Bookkeeping Talk.* Your client is pleasantly surprised when the company gives her a year's free subscription to the magazine.

Finally, choose the best practices from your personal arsenal of information and tips. Streamline the presentation; simplify things for your client. Boil everything down to the essentials but make sure that nothing pertinent is left out. As with information overload, don't overwhelm. Micro-tactics that might be called for in for the future are best left for the future or handled on an on-call, need-to-know basis.

A Consultant should heed certain guidelines.

Here are a few practical guidelines for the *Consultant* role:

- Choose the setting carefully. It should be non-confrontational for the other person, in purpose, and quiet. If you're consulting with an individual at work, make sure that this activity doesn't breech organizational policy or protocol. Allow enough time for each session.

- Keep the sessions confidential, and assure client of privacy.

- Keep your questions low key and watch your phrasing. The questions you ask should be non-threatening and non-challenging, indicating that you have a sincere interest in helping the other person resolve the situation.

- In discussions, seek common ground. Look into your own background and experiences for things the client can relate to his or her own situation.

- Be attentive to the other person and make sure to listen. Rephrasing in your own words what the client has told you will help clarify the issue.

- If you encounter situations that are beyond your ability to help, inform the client and suggest an alternative route for problem resolution.

Key Points in the Chapter

In the *Consultant* role, your job is to help clarify concerns, facilitate for the client as he or she faces and comes to grips with his or her feelings about the situation, to explore options with the client, and assist as he or she person in arrives at a solution. Certain behaviors will help you do this. For instance, conducting a SWOT analysis will allow the client or other person to explore his or her goals and inner feelings about the situation and to examine the external environment objectively. Make sure to provide the client with useful information relative to the situation, but avoid overwhelming with content. By following certain guidelines such as seeking common ground, you can assist the client in seeking resolution for a problematic situation.

CHAPTER SIX

PITCHMAN/PITCHWOMAN

When persuasion to a "yes" is the priority.

In 1914, following the Ludlow, Colorado, state militia massacre of striking coal miners, the public currency of millionaire industrialist and mine owner John D. Rockefeller plummeted. One of the iconic American "robber barons" of the early 20th Century and the richest man in the world, Rockefeller and other tycoons of the time pursued a public-be-damned philosophy of business, their actions ruthless, harsh, uncaring, and profit-driven. It fell to Ivy Lee, the first professional public relations man in history, to restore public confidence and trust in Rockefeller industries by persuading him that there was a better way to conduct business than by making his millions on the backs of largely immigrant mine workers and ruthlessly calling in the armed state militia to keep them in line.

Like Lee, some people are influential by nature; others are not. However, persuasion is a learned art, and by following the concepts in this chapter, you can learn how to effectively pitch an idea, a concept, a program, so that it gets the "yes" of adoption. There's a strategy to persuasion. Unlike the tactics of a carnival barker, it must be employed subtly. But to employ it successfully, you first have to understand the other person's hot-button needs and the underlying ones as well.

Case history number one

An African American couple who celebrate Kwanza each year refuse to be interviewed by a reporter for the metro newspaper even though the editor had set it up. "We've changed our mind," said the elderly man. "We're not interested." As the reporter, you just drove 30 miles for the interview. In addition, you're on noon deadline and your photographer will arrive shortly to photograph the couple in typical African dress. How do you approach this? Call your editor and indicate failure? Persuade the couple to change their mind? Your response: *Pitchman/ Pitchwoman.*

Case history number two

A line manager at a glass-container manufacturing plant has just learned that the corporation's R & D division has researched the feasibility of manufacturing aluminum cans for the same purpose. He stops you in the hall and wants to know why. "Aluminum cans are lightweight, sure, but glass containers have always been valued for keeping their contents fresher." As plant manager, you have the answer to his question, and the R & D figures to back it up. Your response? *Pitchman/ Pitchwoman.*

But how do you approach the situation? First, choose a mutually acceptable time and place to sit down with your partner and map out the full scope of the short-term and long-term benefits to him, the corporation, and to his employees on the production line if the plant goes to aluminum cans. Make sure to prioritize those benefits according to your partner's concerns. In conversation, draw out those concerns. It's obvious that he has some very real fears: "Could the plant be shut down? Then what about layoffs while the plant retools?" He's also concerned about learning a new technology and having to teach it to his line employees. "Could I lose my job? Would they bring in someone else to do it? Could some of my employees be fired?" Fears like this and the other person's lack of confidence in his ability constitute obstacles. In order to persuade your partner to a yes, you have to overcome them. Parry each of his objections one by one. Don't exhort—you're not a preacher or a carnival pitchman—but answer them factually, using the information you have in hand from R&D and sales figure projections to show him how retooling for aluminum can production *will build on his successes*. Be solution-focused. Draw out each of your partner's objections, then reframe them in a positive light using not only words, but tone of voice, spirit, and body language.

Your partner shakes his head. "I don't like it," he says. "Sure, there's some benefits to going aluminum, I can see that. But the company is the largest manufacturer of glass containers in the world, and I can't see us losing our reputation." You ask yourself, is this really what he's concerned about? Our company's reputation? It's obvious your partner hasn't shifted gears to be curious about the situation. Your response: Very carefully, very subtly, awaken anticipatory regret in your partner should the company fail to retool for the higher-demand aluminum cans. Gingerly create a mental experience for him, an image of what could result from the company's failure to capitalize on the benefits of aluminum cans. Above all, re-image the situation on a positive note of hope.

Identity meditation

It's obvious to you that the middle manager received his initial information about retooling for aluminum cans from an informal, unofficial source. You could see the frown lines on his forehead and almost hear the internal dialogue as he mentally scratched his head in self-talk confusion: "This can't be happening. This can't be happening. I'll have to go find another job." It's your job to handle it, lest the situation get out of hand and spread to the line workers. Your best choice for identity meditation shouldn't involve panic. As plant manager and in this case pitchman, you've dealt with the public before, both internally and externally. You know how to talk their language and respond to their needs. You know how to proceed from objectives, and how to parry objections by meeting them factually and reframing the situation positively. In fact, you're socially credible. Your identity meditation could be, "I have a track record of success in working with people and satisfying their needs." While this is a tight situation, you've just overcome your own self-talk gremlins.

Skillful communication is vital

To become a skilled persuader, you need to communicate effectively one on one and in group. Study the speeches of John F. Kennedy ("*Ich bin ein Berliner*"), Winston Churchill ("Our finest hour"), and Marc Anthony ("Friends, Romans, Countrymen"). Note that while the speaker seems to be addressing each of us individually, he includes all of us in the situation. Persuasive people rely on such inclusiveness. They know how to employ both verbal and nonverbal communication to create and convey meaning. They create empathy in a variety of ways, sharing with the other person the doubts, the fears, the confusion that they themselves initially felt. Frame your words, posture, gestures, voice for a positive response. That means being positive yourself; for example, rather than speak of *troubles*, speak instead of *solutions*, rather than be *anti*-littering, be *pro*-recycling. The techniques you choose should mirror the style your partner or other listeners use and are accustomed to. For instance, using the same gestures or arm movements as your partner builds on the empathy you've created verbally. A few tips can help:

- Don't shout or speed up in panic. Use a modulated, well-paced voice, one that reflects your confidence.

- Establish common ground before pitching your message. Use words such as "we" rather than "I" or "me." This can build a relationship that includes your partner in the new mission.

- Mentally assume your partner's attitudinal mindset about proposed changes before proceeding. This allows you to choose your words and develop a persuasive strategy.

- Make sure to use words familiar to your partner. Avoid new terminologies that will put you into the role of teacher.

- Listen even more than you speak and avoid teaching or preaching.

- Watch out for using the other person's name over and over; reserve use of the name for important points you're making.

- Use positive body language. This can involve arms unfolded, legs uncrossed or at least open in the direction of the other person, the space between you nonthreatening for the culture and conventional for the type of conversation. Don't let your gaze wander from the other person; maintain eye contact. And make sure that if appropriate to the particular situation, you use a firm handshake.

- Select certain motivational words that will help persuade the other person to your point of view. Use these words judiciously, but throughout the conversation. For example, "right now" is active and preferable to "now" or "today." Or "annual bonus for higher achievement" rather than "extra pay for the additional responsibility." Listen to your intuition for guidance. That way, you'll notice those words to which your partner responds positively and those that get a negative response and should be avoided.

Remember that you can make more progress in conversation by asking questions that produce a "yes" response.

- Keep focused on the results you want, but make sure to translate the benefits of a proposed change into terms that are meaningful to the other person; for example, into increased salary.

The action element

Now clinch your pitch. Insure your objectives are met by persuading the other person to take specific action on your proposal or message. In the case of the African American couple, persuade them to don African dress and lay out the Kwanza table decorations. For the dubious middle manager, request he choose team leaders for the proposed new production lines or that he investigate the public benefits of recycling aluminum containers compared to the heavier glass ones. If necessary, set a deadline for completion of these tasks. The action should not be a deal breaker but should include clear and specific tasks that will indicate commitment. Why? Because research has shown that people who have an opportunity for exposure through a trial run are more likely to adopt the proposal, program, concept, or message.

Key Points in the Chapter

There's a better way to pitch points than carnival barkers use. Persuading others to adopt an attitude, idea, concept, or program involves the subtle use of communication strategies that often involve mirroring the communication methods most comfortable to your partner or listeners. Getting to the "yes" of adoption means you first have to discover the hot-button and underlying needs and fears of the other person, then one by one dismantle the obstacles by prioritizing how certain benefits will satisfy those needs. If the other person still doesn't seem sufficiently curious, carefully and gently awaken anticipatory regret should the attitude, idea, concept, or program not be acted on. In touchy situations, it's essential to repeat to yourself an identity meditation that is not only credible but effective in chasing away your own self-talk gremlins.

CHAPTER SEVEN

ALLY

To assert in meaningful ways that the partnership goes beyond immediate interests and even comes before personal gain.

"If there is trouble, I stay here to help you. For your father—for your father."

Enzo Aguello, baker from Sicily, speaks to Michael Corleone and offers to protect the hospitalized Don Corleone from would-be assassins.

In the 1972 iconic flick *The Godfather,* Enzo, the Sicilian baker, risked his life to stand guard outside the hospital where Don Corleone lay recovering from bullet wounds. Enzo's offer was one of grateful thanks to Corleone for preventing his deportation to Sicily after World War II. This exchange of dialogue illustrates the next role in the relationship process: *Ally*. Enzo was demonstrating that the relationship with the Don went far beyond his immediate interests, far beyond self-preservation—and that it came before personal gain.

Have you ever acted as *Ally*? Have you ever wished you had one? While not a guardian angel but occasionally similar to an *amicus curiae,* an *Ally* may support you or your position, stand up for you in delicate interactions, or facilitate a solution when you're blocked from carrying out some action or doing your assigned job correctly. Most of us have at least a small cadre of personal allies; some of those are people who have helped chart our course success by keeping us focused on the tasks at hand and helping to clarify our objectives. In fact, two current TV sitcoms are all about creating allies: *Burn Notice* and *Suits*. Anyone can act as *Ally*. For instance:

Willa Howe, an unemployed and experienced associate professor, was hired into a lower-grade position at a small college in the Southwest. Expecting the usual good behavior she received from students at a brick-and-mortar school, Howe was shocked when students began loudly complaining in class about her teaching, hurling insults at her, and denigrating the course content. As the weeks went by and student attendance in the class shrank, Howe finally threw in the towel. Using the latest methods, she had done all she could to teach the class. Howe packed up her books and notes. Leaving the students behind, she walked out of the classroom and almost immediately into the arms of the assistant dean passing by in the hall. An experienced teacher and administrator at that school, the assistant dean was a woman with whom she'd previously established a comfortable relationship. Hearing the story of classroom abuse, the assistant dean decided to take matters in hand. She accompanied Howe back to the classroom. Kindly but firmly, she not only insisted on ethical classroom behavior in the future but point by point went over each objective in the course, showing students how the professor was meeting them. In supporting Howe, the assistant dean had slipped into a new role: *Ally*.

The public affairs director of a Fortune 100 corporation headquartered in your metropolitan area was approached by the art teacher at a large high school, asking if her students could exhibit their works on the walls of the corporate lobby. The director knew that the CEO frowned on artwork of any type displaced on the walls. However, he saw some merit in the idea of giving local students additional exposure. Although the move would carry some personal risk to his job, he decided to go to bat for the students. He became the art teacher's *Ally*. That move could only work, however, if he himself secured an *Ally* in the CEO's secretary, herself a supporter of local art.

The sales manager at Crocker Corporation believed the marketing collateral being produced by the graphic arts team was too stale and dull to appeal to the younger demographic of the company's market. Repeated discussions with the graphics team leader, however, produced only a "we'll try" when it came to improvement. The sales manager was stumped. Sales figures were falling, a matter that reflected on his ability. Deciding to take a risk, he approached the vice president of sales with a controversial suggestion: Send key graphics arts staffers back to school for an upgrading of their abilities. Expecting to hear that it would be too expensive and too costly in man hours, he found a surprising *Ally* in the very person who headed the lackluster graphics arts team: the team leader, who himself put his job at risk to support the proposal.

A structural engineer on multiple building projects was drawing a hefty $15,000 a month when the bottom fell out of the economy. Without an income and having failed to save for such eventuality, he and his wife sold their two cars, transferred their children from private to public school, applied for welfare, and both spent hours each day tirelessly looking for work. Eventually, his wife found a part-time job as a kindergarten aide, but the structural engineer continued to look, finding it more and more difficult to cold call for jobs when they were 20 to 40 miles away. One day, he attended a local Chamber of Commerce meeting where he and several others in a similar position discussed the problems they were experiencing. The following morning, he had a phone call. "My husband and I heard you speak at the Chamber of Commerce meeting yesterday," said a woman's voice at the other end. "We know what you're going through. You can't properly look for work if you don't have a car. My husband and I are going to buy you one."

Behaving as an Ally

An *Ally* exhibits certain classic behaviors:

- An *Ally* doesn't seek out thanks but discreetly discovers the opposing interests and the arguments behind them.
- An *Ally* defends the client's goals in a concrete manner, using logic and facts to abut the opposing organizational interests or those of another party.
- Although a sacrifice may be involved, the *Ally* doesn't compromise needlessly nor second-guess himself or herself.
- The *Ally* employs a light touch, not a heavy-handed one, when conveying to the client any personal cost or risk involved in assuming the *Ally* role.

In short, the *Ally* takes responsibility for seeing the situation through without seeking thanks or expecting congratulations.

An *Ally* is partly a relationship artist. He or she designs the action to be taken, the success to be enjoyed, and the stress that may accompany the process so that each of these aligns with those of the client. Part of becoming an *Ally* involves drawing on your own experience. For example, the late Judith Benninger Brown, an attorney, was Florida's first white civil rights activist. A victim of childhood abuse, she applied the lessons she'd learned from it to her work on behalf of others. Jailed several times for allying African Americans, she next took up the cause of abused spouses on the run. Like Brown, when acting as *Ally*, make sure to tap into what you've learned from your own experiences; from that informed position, apply those lessons to your client's situation.

Building Ally relationships

How can you build *Ally* relationships, particularly with the people you value most?

- First, from your own experiences with oppression, isolate those individuals who allied you in your past times of need. Make a list of them. Which character traits did they have in common? Compassion? Commitment? Selflessness? Motivation? Independent thought? Knowledge? Now make a list of those people with whom you'd like to build ally relationships. By increasing your knowledge of these people and building the necessary character traits, you'll discover the ways an *Ally* can assist when such assistance may be needed. By becoming a knowledgeable person with a reputation for competent performance, you, too, can be the *Ally* called on in times of stress or even crisis.

- Second, examine your self-talk gremlins. They say something like this: "Oh, no, I can't. *Ally* the CFO? *Ally* my teacher? Befriend the postal worker?" Right now, you're beset by doubts and fears. You're afraid to take the risk. And you don't think you'll be effective enough. Really? Who better than you, an understanding and compassionate person, to step up to the plate for these people? Do you really think that being compassionate, committed, and informed will detract somehow from your performance, your personhood? Your identity meditation can be simply, "I'm a good and understanding person."

- Third, wear another pair of glasses. If you want to build an *Ally* relationship with Sue, for example, you need to adopt her perspective in order to see and understand the needs and concerns that drive her.

- Fourth, to be consistently supportive of your partner or a cause, you'll need to be committed to your own personal growth.

Ally behaviors differ from person to person, situation to situation. Some people choose to ally themselves with groups that espouse such social causes as poverty. Others are situational allies, standing up for someone else when the need arises. In either case, an *Ally* must be prepared to take some personal risks and often must go against the public or corporate tide.

When alliances conflict

In choosing to *Ally* herself with those targeted for discrimination and to respond to their needs, Judith Benninger Brown, the attorney, broke fealty with long-time friends and colleagues with whom she shared identity. As an *Ally*, she clearly ran afoul of many prejudices and traditions held by others. Their failure to understand such dedication, however, was partly hers. She made a major mistake by not explaining clearly to others the nature of the discrimination she had chosen to fight and the overarching importance of getting everyone allied to the cause.

Don't make the same mistake. A television ad, for example, positions itself as our *Ally*—as being "on our side," and "working for us." Yet this is not a dialogic relationship and one to which we can give immediate, one-on-one feedback. Build your *Ally* relationship by listening closely to your partner with the intention of really understanding. Listen intently, listen with heart, then clearly and reasonably communicate the facts of a situation to another person or to others. Remember that your role should not be adversarial: Your purpose is not to defend, not to antagonize, but to support. Only by building trust in this fashion can you establish a sound ally relationship.

Key Points in the Chapter

To be a successful *Ally* requires you develop understanding, wisdom, compassion and the ability to clearly communicate the facts of a situation to another. To serve as *Ally*, you have to see a situation through the eyes of the other person and understand the needs and concerns that drive him or her. In choosing to be an *Ally*, you automatically accept certain risks, risk that can jeopardize your job or alienate peers or supervisors. Start out by listing those people from your past who have allied you. Note the character traits they have in common, then deliberately work at developing those traits in yourself.

CHAPTER EIGHT

FRIEND

To connect on the level of human affection and interest apart from all work goals and professional expectations.

Do you have a friend at work? Are you one? Many employers these days believe that workplace friendships are beneficial, that they build company loyalty. Such closeness among staffers, they say, is beneficial to teamwork because it increases productivity. In fact, a recent *Randstad Work Watch* survey indicated that two-thirds of the people surveyed say that friends at work makes the job more enjoyable; more than half reported that friends make their job more satisfying. Are you willing to be the voice of reason when necessary and the echo of passion for a friend's ideas and dreams? Will you be present for your friend when he or she feels vulnerable, stressed out?

The responsibility for being a true friend shouldn't be dismissed lightly. On or off the job, friendship carries both commitment and responsibility. That's why you'll sometimes find yourself wondering if it wouldn't be easier simply to step into the role of consultant or ally. After all, you might convince yourself, isn't it more objective? Doesn't it carry less responsibility? Isn't it less risky? The answer is "yes" to all three. But in the scenarios below, only the role of "friend" applies, and your identity meditation may be simply "Friends go the extra mile."

- A friend at work asks you to cover for him while he takes an extra hour today for lunch. Would you cover for him when it jeopardizes your own work?

- A friend at the bloodmobile has to rush home because her daughter is ill. She asks you to take charge and draw blood from the people lined up to donate. As the intake supervisor, you haven't drawn blood for years. In fact, you're not even vetted on some of the new equipment. Will you be willing to help out?

- A workplace friend in the computer software company where you both work is being ridiculed about his choice of clothing. It happens at the lunch table with the entire team present. Do you stand up for him?

Unwritten principles of friendship

There are certain unwritten principles to maintaining a solid friendship. You must:

- Be accepting of the other person and unwavering in loyalty.

- Accept personal responsibility for your part of the relationship.

- Be a good listener and when called for, a rephraser of ideas and a paraphraser of comments as well.

- Be supportive of the other person but at the same time, unafraid to offer unbiased criticism when it's called for. Giving advice, offering direction—if truly heartfelt—is the hallmark of a good friend.

- Be willing to go beyond sympathy and to empathize, to actually feel the other's pain or distress. When a co-worker has lost someone close and is grieving, make sure to reach out to him or her. Let your friend feel the sorrow without being judgmental, let your co-worker know you are there to listen and to help.
- Be available to offer a fresh perspective on a situation or scenario.
- Show love. To be a friend, you have to find in yourself a genuine affection for the other person and be able to express it. You not only exhibit a desire to spend time with the other person, but you're willing to share your own experiences to show that you understand and can identify.
- Understand that friendship doesn't need good deeds reciprocated. As a friend, you champion the other person and talk up your friend's good points to others. You challenge and stimulate, doing what it takes to help him or her succeed.
- Respect privacy. You may want to assert yourself and offer suggestions or comments on your friend's personal or work life, but don't tread on privacy. Be observant and learn in which situations your comments would be welcomed and when they would not.
- Understand that a true friend is always there, challenging and stimulating, talking up the friend's good points to others.

You must do all this without compromising your own values and ideas. Boundaries are important; make sure you maintain them. For example, avoid sharing so much personal information and in such depth that one accidental slip from the other person can compromise your good standing among others. Make sure to draw the line between professional commitments and friendships at work. Co-worker cliques can cause jealousy, affect productivity, and even contribute to the breakup of the team. In particular, watch out for becoming overly friendly with a supervisor or boss.

Case history

The newest faculty member in the communications department at a southern university was delighted when the department director, also a female, became chummy with her. They'd share lunch together, stop to chat in the halls, and sometimes "double date" with their husbands for dinner or attend some outside event in which all four had a mutual interest. As the friendship continued to warm up both on and off the job, a clique of male and female coworkers in the department felt they were being overlooked in decision-making. Sensing what had become a negative workplace culture, the department director pulled back from the friendship. Unfortunately, the animosity and distrust of the newcomer didn't abate. Her students even picked up on the snide comments of other faculty members, and the atmosphere in her classes quickly turned negative. In time, the new faculty member became so uncomfortable on the job that she resigned.

When a friendship from the workplace turns sour like this and divides and disrupts, what should you do? Clearly, collaboration has suffered, and efforts to teach successfully have been undermined. The solution is not so clear. Both newcomer and department director must share responsibility for failing to establish a balance between socializing and working. In addition, their chumminess at work was very visible: They were seen frequently socializing in the halls with each other and lunching together on campus. By failing to keep an appropriate distance between supervisor and faculty member, the department director eroded her authority, and both women left themselves open to gossip and claims of favoritism. In addition, their interactions telegraphed to other faculty members that it was acceptable to behave the same way.

The premise of such TV sitcoms as *Mad Men, Friends,* and *Seinfeld* provide a window for viewing friendships. Having good friends at work is a strong support system for weathering the highs and lows. Work becomes more enjoyable, you become happier. You're not only more engaged in what you're doing, you're doing it better because your creative juices are flowing. Once you're comfortable with what you're doing and the people you're doing it with, you'll be able to solve problems and find new approaches to them. And as a bonus, when you're stressed out or angry about something, you'll have friends who understand and won't mind your venting your frustrations.

Water-cooler friends

Even though many career experts believe that a staffer puts out more team effort in a socially inclusive environment, some employers *discourage* close friendships at work, calling the friends "water-cooler partners." Said the manager of a large office-supply store: "Close friendships on the job encourages socializing, and that interferes with productivity and customer service." In a variation, the friendship between a boss and a subordinate can cause jealousy among other team members; it also risks compromising the potential for unbiased criticism of a project or solution. And if you're too chummy with one or more co-workers, say experts, it may portray you as not serious about career advancement. Such a work environment is at least partly reflective of a military situation. Commissioned officers don't socialize with non-coms, and even non-coms prefer to socialize with each other rather than with lower-level enlisted personnel. While dating and certainly marriage among the ranks is acceptable, the military forbids socializing and marriage between officers and enlisted personnel.

Nevertheless, you need at least one friend at work—someone in an otherwise impersonal environment who will push you to achieve, cheer you up when you're low or with good humor pick you up when you feel you've failed. In fact, a recent Gallup Q12 employee engagement survey revealed that having friends at work—the kind of people who won't play politics with you—is a predictor of your success. It keeps you engaged in the workplace, enhances your well-being, reduces workplace stress, and helps you maintain good health and a positive outlook. On the plus side for employers, workplace friendships not only increase productivity and profits but build loyalty and employee retention. As well, the Gallup survey revealed that engaged employees have managers who care about them personally and value their opinion.

If you're a manager or team leader

You've been promoted out of your team to teamwork supervisor. In this capacity as manager, you'll be walking a fine line. You've made a few strong friends on that team; now you're leading them. How do you handle work and friendships when they're your subordinates? Without compromising professionalism, you can still enjoy camaraderie with your friends who are team members. Laugh with them, joke with them. Don't be too hard on them; don't be too lenient with them. Above all, don't automatically assume that your friends will understand. That's why you'll want to talk with them away from work about the new situation. But do remember to keep boundaries: Your comments and behavior should be appropriate to the work situation. In addition, remember that it takes two to maintain a relationship. Those on the team who are your friends may feel just as awkward in the new situation as you. To keep them as friends without distancing yourself, be patient. Spend extra effort off the job on nurturing that friendship, but not at the expense of compromising your professionalism or incurring jealousies.

Intuition and the unwritten principles of friendship

You want your bloodmobile friend to be there for her daughter. Yet initially you felt that intuition was telling you to refuse her request. In this situation, it's helpful to remember that intuition is not talking but instead the self-talk gremlins of fear and uncertainty. Remember the unwritten principles of friendship: "As a friend, you champion the other person and do what it takes to help him or her succeed."

Your friend asks you to cover for him while he takes an extra hour at lunch. Intuitively, you feel that it's wrong to do so, that it compromises your values. Does it? Or does this principle apply: "Be supportive of the other person and unwavering in loyalty." A quick mental check has assured you that your friend is neither flippant nor irresponsible. You agree to his request without probing for the reason behind the longer lunch.

When your friend was ridiculed for his clothing at lunch you remembered the principle of "a true friend is always there, challenging and stimulating, talking up a friend's good points to others" and you spoke to the team.

Key Points in the Chapter

Having friends at work can benefit your career goals, but overstepping boundaries by being too chummy or intimate can kayo your standing with others. A recent Gallup survey revealed that friends keep you engaged in the workplace, enhance your well-being and health, reduce stress, and contribute to a positive outlook in the workplace. The same can be said of friends in life. Workplace friendships also increase productivity and employee retention. Unfortunately, a certain percentage of employers discourage socializing at work, believing it to be unprofitable for the company. Of the ten unwritten principles of friendship, the seventh—show love—may be the hardest. You can cultivate it by working on trust and empathy.

CHAPTER NINE

TRANSITIONING BETWEEN ROLES

Are you an opportunist? A quick-change artist? Do you pride yourself on rapid role sequencing, casting one off, trying on another to fit the situation at any given moment? A warning: To establish relationships that work, role transitioning should not be as easy as changing your tie or your scarf or your cap to fit the moment. Whether *Ally*, *Consultant*, *Friend*, *Change Agent*, *Pitchman* or *Pitchwoman*, to be meaningful and genuine, the role you assume at any given moment not only depends on the cues you get from the other person but—equally as important—on the relationship you normally have with a particular individual and the degree of flexibility within it. In most cases, you'll pre-plan with an end role in mind—this is particularly true if you're in sales—but you may have to adopt one or more transitional roles before assuming it. For example:

- You step into an industrial customer's office by appointment and immediately adopt the *Pitchman* role without hearing and seeing two essential clues: The client is distracted; his daughter is in intensive care. Should you forge ahead anyway? Will you be successful? You bite your lip. You realize you'll have to back-burner the *Pitchman* role for a transitional one—*Ally* or *Friend*, depending on the flexibility of your established relationship with the customer. Whether you're able to assume the *Pitchman* role on this appointment will depend, again, on the clues you receive next from your customer.

- As a manager, you've just given a team leader some feedback on an important project report she turned in. You want to use the *Change Agent* role at this point because there are substantive errors of logic and organization in the written report. The team leader acknowledges this but says she doesn't know how to change it. Immediately you assume the *Consultant* role.

Caught off balance

In any given situation, the existing relationship between you and a co-worker, boss, teacher, client/customer, or friend, together with the clues you receive from the other person, will govern whether you initially have to assume an intermediate role or can move swiftly to the target end role without pause. This is particularly true in a fast-paced, multi-tasking world where situations change quickly and often demand fairly rapid adjustments that—just as often—may prove faulty. Sometimes, you'll be caught off balance. For example, you commiserate with a team leader who just had a nasty public spat with the supervisor. You pat her on the back with understanding and suggest that the two of you have a drink together after work. Unfortunately, you've just come across as an opportunist. She's the team leader, you're a member of the team; your positions are not co-equal. What would have been the proper transitional role? *Ally*.

Case history

You assemble your team in the conference room this morning to discuss motivation. As *Change Agent*, you haven't brought up this topic before but you're doing it now because you've seen little improvement in productivity in the six months you've been team leader. You open the discussion with a well-known analogy of the "little train that could." Harold, your creative point man, snorts: "That's bull. We work on much greater tasks than that." Emily, your mathematician, chimes in defensively: "I agree. You just don't see all the work we put into each project."

You quickly realize that neither person is open to change. Being stonewalled by both Harold and Emily could soon be mirrored in the rest of the team. With a silent identity meditation, you shift the focus slightly and assume the role of *Consultant* (teacher). "Emily, how many man-hours do you estimate it would take to complete our new project?" As Emily computes it, you turn to Harold. "Harold, how many man-hours do you estimate that you, Fred, and D'Arcy put in on both parts of the project we just finished?" The three quickly put their heads together and come up with an estimate. You turn back to Emily. "As our efficiency expert, Emily, if you divide our new project into smaller parts, where can we shave off 15 minutes a day—that's one-and-a-half hours per week? If we do our work efficiently, we can use the extra time to collaborate on something truly creative." All eyes are now on Emily, who has your attention as an *Ally*.

Role sequencing

No matter how many colors to which a chameleon can change, at base it's still a chameleon: We expect it to change colors. However, changing roles at work to meet the demands of a situation can fail to build trust if it's seen as transparent and self-serving. The basis of any relationship is the respect, perhaps even love and affection, two people have for each other. Only by understanding the other's perspective and building a relationship of honesty and fairness can role sequencing work to meet a desired end. Remember also that the purpose of assuming other roles is as much to meet the needs of another person as it is your own. Evaluate the situation for its potential: Avoid role-sequencing if it won't be worth it.

In the pre-planning stage, decide the purpose of a particular role adoption and how it will fit into the larger scheme of things. Develop a step-by-step and perhaps role-by-role plan for getting there. Now image the outcome; rehearse it mentally. Be sure to plan for contingencies along the way that may force you to assume intermediate roles; image yourself in those roles also and anticipate the reaction you may encounter. Good contingency plans will measure your success. They can keep you from bulling ahead, making missteps, and never reaching your target role. Finally, decide how you're going to handle yourself in the situation and image the other person playing a part. In determining the other person's interests and needs, try mentally rehearsing the roles: Put yourself in the place of your partner and gauge the likely reaction.

The transitioning process follows a simple procedure after pre-planning. First, listen and watch for indicators—those words and actions that will you clue you into a role. Remember that verbal messages in themselves won't convey feelings; only by paying close attention to the speaker and feeding back his or her message in your own words will you demonstrate to the other person that you understand. Make sure to pay attention to the response you get. Next, evoke an identity meditation. Finally, don't press ahead with your own agenda: Follow your intuition. Remember that the way you express a particular role should be honestly felt and an outgrowth of your character.

Key Points in the Chapter

Chameleons change color when they're attacked or feel fearful. Your purpose in role transitioning, however, is to meet your partner's felt need, and you have to do it honestly, with respect. The role to which you transition at any given time is based on the verbal and visual cues you get from the other person as well as on the history of the relationship and the degree of flexibility in it. Different situations require different roles. Temporarily relinquishing your original role preference, and being flexible in transitioning among the roles, will govern your success. Although you may have to transition through one or more roles before getting to your target role, remember that you're meeting the needs of someone else and building trust as you go along.

CHAPTER TEN

EFFECTIVE COMMUNICATION

Whether you're communicating with customers and clients or internally, with members of your work force, you'll be wise to match certain communication styles to each person's personality type. This technique is particularly effective as you assume different roles. For example:

- Emily from the previous chapter is known to be efficient and data-oriented. A typical personality type ST, she'll be turned off if you brainstorm ideas with no practical outcome. Why? Because Emily appreciates information that is factual, credible, and relevant to the situation at hand.

- You, on the other hand, are a balanced NF. You're an idealist. Unlike Emily, you expect your work to be enjoyable. You're a brainstormer, filled with new insights and perspectives. You dislike extensive paperwork and are turned off by people at work who play politics. You work best by keying off other idealists, yet you need Emily and others of similar personality type to be the cogs to your wheels and keep the projects going day to day. Your forte is the ability to encourage growth in others, and that makes you a good manager.

Since the late 1800s, social psychologists have sought to isolate personality types and apply them to everyday living. Of course, no one is exclusively one type/temperament or another, and by the mid-1900s, the team of Isabel Briggs Myers and her mother Katharine Briggs had developed a method for bracketing personality into four functioning pairs—a Type S with a Type F, for example, or a Type S paired with a Type T. In combination, each pair exhibits certain personality characteristics that we can apply to communication and role interpretation. Thus, if an NT co-worker, for example—the big-picture-oriented element on the work team—needed to communicate successfully with an ST (Emily), the co-worker would have to be businesslike, demonstrate greater responsibility than usual, and avoid taking up Emily's time with irrelevant detail and pleasantries.

By understanding personality typologies, you'll develop the insight needed to motivate, influence, lead, teach, and help others. You'll become more adaptable to different situations, and this will leverage your influence when transitioning between roles. For some people, however, adaptability doesn't come easily and requires patience and understanding to become more flexible. Were you a Type ST, or Emily personality, for example, you'd become upset when work you assigned is turned in sub-standard and has to be re-done. On the other hand, an NF personality experiences conflict when some of the team members violate the code of ethics and cut corners dishonestly. Since D'Arcy, an NF team member, sees the big picture but likes work to be fun and enjoyable, the best way to connect with her is through idealism and by finding the fun in it. Remember that D'Arcy is concerned with her professional growth and will expect you to help.

When relating with Emily, be businesslike and demonstrate your responsibility. Focus on messages that are factual and credible. Don't linger on pleasantries: Be brief. Emily, an ST, doesn't like surprises. Harold, the NT personality on the team, experiences conflict when the principles developed for a project are faulty; he focuses on the pros and cons of it all. To connect with Harold, quickly establish your credibility, then just as quickly prepare to be challenged. Make sure to let him draw his own conclusions after the situation has been presented him. Fred is an SF personality—pretty businesslike, practical, results-oriented. Things have to make sense for him, and being shown examples help. He's very centered on building relationships with you and team members. Let Fred know you value his input and give him the opportunity for hands-on experience. Be friendly and spend some time with him on relationship-building. Fred likes people to work together well and gets upset when they disagree.

Each of the functional personality types has different goals. Emily's is efficiency; you'd expect her strong points to be accountability and control. Harold's is mastery of whatever project he's working on; a long-range thinker, Harold designs theoretical concepts for the team. Fred's main goal is to help others, and this makes him not only an excellent team member but effective as well in customer service. D'Arcy, however, needs to feel empowered; she likes creative work that contributes to her growth. Adapt your approach to each functional type even if it means back-burning your own goal for a while.

Flawed communication

More often than not, conflict arises from faulty communication. For this reason, confirm your understanding of what your partner has said by summarizing and feeding it back appropriately. Remember that you don't have to agree with your partner's assessment of a situation. Not at all. But you do have to validate it as being sensible and in the situation, even reasonable. Only by validating someone else's assessment—even if you disagree—have you a platform for continuing the dialogue.

How well do you listen? Emily may be a Type ST, you may be an NT, but she's likely to sense your interest in her work if she believes you're listening to her. Remember that good listening behavior gives you a leg up on your goals: It establishes a connection between you and the other person. Some mistakes you can make in failing to listen:

- I can read your mind. (Jumping in and finishing the sentence before the other person can.)
- Forging ahead and refusing to acknowledge an emotional situation or reaction.
- I can go you one better. (Imposing your idea on the other person's without hearing it out thoroughly.)
- Interpreting silence as a void to be immediately filled.
- "Talking through" and overriding the other person.
- Telegraphing your inattentiveness by multitasking at the same time.
- Using dismissive body language—even tone of voice—that indicates your lack of interest or respect for the other person's thoughts.

If your verbal message to a partner says one thing, but your body language doesn't agree, you're telegraphing insincerity. Unfold your arms, if your legs are crossed keep them open toward your partner, and maintain eye contact. By establishing this position of openness, you'll encourage a dialogue with the other person. Make sure to maintain the proper space between each of you for the situation.

In addition, it helps to check in periodically on your relationship with co-workers. That way, you can review the relationship and make necessary changes. If you need to apologize, do it now and do it honestly. Don't lose the opportunity to keep communicating with other people: It's also a way of helping you monitor the relationship. If issues loom with a co-worker that need to be resolved, don't put them on hold. Resolve them together. Remember that as a co-worker, as a team member or leader, as a manager or supervisor, you're expected to be accountable for the choices you make and the activities you undertake: Your behavior will be emulated by others. However, putting off decisions will only erode your influence.

A few constructive tips for communicating with others

Different personality types have different styles of communication. Private people, for example, guard their thoughts jealously; garrulous people on your team may over-talk. A few communication tips may ease the way:

- In communicating your thoughts to others, incorporate feedback from co-workers in both your thinking and discussion. Incorporating feedback creates opportunities for collaboration.

Make feedback constructive—don't personalize it—but take into account how others may feel.

- Don't ignore conflicts or personal issues, and don't hesitate to deal with them promptly.
- Be sensitive to personality differences. Don't intrude on the lives of others or seek personal information they may not want to share.
- Develop patience and empathy. Be encouraging, but be aware of differences in work and communication styles.
- Don't expect others to read your mind or to carry out responsibilities you haven't told them about. Communicate clearly.

Key Points in the Chapter

Paying attention to personality types and modifying your approach accordingly will pay off in both the short and the long run. This method is particularly effective when you role sequence. How you choose to communicate with others will either erode your influence or enhance it. If you're a leader, remember that subordinates will emulate your behavior. If you've made poor choices, 'fess up immediately, and encourage dialogue. If you have issues with a co-worker, don't put off resolving them. Deal honestly with people—and make sure to communicate appropriately on both the verbal and nonverbal levels.

CHAPTER ELEVEN

INFLUENCE: IT'S A WRAP

You may have talent, be competent at your job—even proficient—but if you haven't built a network of successful relationships, you lack the influence factor. It's time to get serious about developing your relationship skills because they're the only way you'll develop and wield influence—and keep it.

What is this strange phenomenon that hangs like a veil over people, distinguishing one person's career, ultimately extinguishing another's? Part grit and determination, part ambition and empathy, influence is the combination of three elements working together—amassed wisdom, intuition, and a series of concrete steps that form an influence learning curve when applied. The need to understand the social psychology of influence and its many facets is crucial because competition is not only increasing locally and worldwide, it has become more aggressive. Crises are resulting in the world partly because of a failure to ethically influence behavior.

Influencing people—getting them to change their minds—can be a tough task. Yet as a compliance professional, you have to understand the influence mosaic, those sources and drivers of influence that allow you to identify and anticipate resistance to change. In large part, how well you handle resistance to change will reflect how you think about a certain situation or a particular person. For example, if a team leader steps out of his cubicle and asks you to help him with some paperwork, what do you do? And how do you handle the customer who's angry because a key product you sold him hasn't arrived yet at his warehouse?

Risk-taker or maintainer of the status quo?

Which defines you: Do you take risks to get expected rewards? Or do you feel it's safer and more balanced to remain on the current path? The choice is yours, and it will influence your ability to ask the key questions and obtain the feedback you need that will link your program, product—perhaps even your idea or innovation—to the values, needs, wishes, maybe even fears of the other person. Should you push your agenda? Remember that it's easier for people to change their minds, even make decisions, if they believe the thought is original with them. Communication provides the most effective way to approach it. Frame your what, how, and follow-up questions by conveying to the other person just how interested you really are in his or her interests, needs, desires, values. Then make sure to give the person a reason to rationally justify a purchase or an action; for example, a reason for donating blood at work.

Hidden messages will influence a person's mind change or decision. Don't put the cart before the horse: The real issue here is not changing someone's mind but changing someone's behavior, and that's not easy to do. Role adoption, role sequencing—these mean nothing unless you first find the hidden content—the backstory and emotion—that motivates the other person's thinking and behavior and is causing the resistance. Chapter One offers several suggestions for countering it.

Are you influential?

You may be in a position of authority, but do you have power or influence? In fact, does power make you a good leader? Authority, leadership, power—these are activated by the relationships struck by a collaborative leader who, in an ideal work environment, inspires others to contribute equally to the common goal. However, people have agendas that may differ from yours as leader. Success will be possible only by harnessing your goal to the sources of influence. Use peer pressure, use rewards and incentives, control the social environment, modify the physical environment, and provide reinforcement in order to influence mindsets and effect the desired behavior change. This is particularly crucial when business is undergoing an organizational change that lowers morale and creates visible resistance.

Influencing the behavior of others carries responsibility. Make sure you act on what you believe, remain positive, give time and attention to others in order to establish rapport, and that you understand the hidden "contracts" of bargains and obligations—the reciprocity factor (see Chapter Two).

How do people make decisions?

Do people act on what they believe to be true? Do they violate it? Do they change their minds? Social psychologists tell us that commitment triggers consistency. For example, an acquaintance of yours bought a female West Highland White Terrier, or Westie, from you, the breeder. Now, a year later, you approach her with a male Westie. Not wishing to appear inconsistent with her earlier purchase from you, she more or less agrees to the sale. But is that the right decision, she worries? Does she really need another dog, particularly a male? That implies a breeding pair. Is she prepared to be a breeder? You invite her to a nearby AKC dog show where she meets other breeders showing Westies and like-minded consumers such as herself.

Personality should also be factored into any influence situation. Keep your attitude positive, your personality likeable, and make sure to demonstrate integrity and competence. Just as people are more comfortable buying products or buying into an idea or suggestion from those who are similar to them in background and appearance, they also tend to buy from people they like. In addition, you can enhance the value of a product or an idea by remembering the rules of advertising: People buy into products, decisions, or opportunities that soon will disappear, are newly scarce, and will be denied them if they don't act now. You can capitalize on this for short-term gains, where emotion rather than logic rules. But to build relationships long-term and demonstrate you have their best interests at heart, it's better to offer co-workers and customers some incentives for something more solid.

Act on cues

What part do you play in a relationship? Is it always consistent? No. The part you play is based in large measure on the verbal and nonverbal cues you receive from your partner. Pay attention to those cues—they'll allow you to negotiate success. They dictate the role you should start with and those you may have to assume on the way to your target goal. Remember that you, too, are providing vocal and nonverbal cues during negotiation. For example, a murmur of assent from you will continue a negotiation but you'll kayo it if your voice is taut with impatience. Standing too far away from the other person when the situation calls for casual intimacy, or inattentively shifting your gaze will destroy the tenor of the moment. While spatial relationships and even the direction of a gaze are specific to the particular culture, if you fail to be congruent in your own verbal and nonverbal behavior—if your smile says one thing, for example, but your posture says another—you'll come across as dishonest, disinterested, even antagonistic.

Reprogramming the voices in your head

"I've tried, but I can never do this right." Is this a self-talk gremlin you've programmed into your head? Or perhaps it's unconscious rather than deliberate. In either event, those nasty voices inside your head that speak of doubts and failure have to be reprogrammed in order for you to take positive action. How can you overcome the negative self-talk in order to proceed? Speak back to those gremlins! Use positive self-talk. Use identity meditations to reprogram your negative habits of thinking and behaving that right now are keeping you stuck in the status quo. An identity meditation—a word, perhaps a phrase—will silently affirm your ability and give you the confidence to move into a new role or transition from one role to another.

The roles

Change Agent

You have five roles from which to choose—*Change Agent, Consultant, Friend, Ally, Pitchman or Pitchwoman.* The role you assume at any given time has to fit the situation and the individual or individuals; the choice can't be arbitrary. Consider the element of change, for example, an ongoing situation in today's fast-paced marketplace. Whether change is opportunistic or assigned, you may first have to transition through one or two other roles to get to that point. If your goal is indeed *Change Agent*, first assess just how ready for a change is your partner, or your team, of even your organization. Is there awareness of the need to change? Has some thought been given to it? Has some action been taken already in that direction? If these clues lead you to a "yes," you're ready to assume the *Change Agent* role. Make sure, however, to do an identity meditation first. If you have been appointed to make changes, draw up a list of S.M.A.R.T. goals before you begin and decide how and when you'll evaluate goal success (see Chapter Four). By successfully handling the *Change Agent* role, you'll have made what was undesirable at the start desirable to everyone concerned without residual bitterness or anger.

Consultant

If you've been cued to mentor another person through words such as "Help," or "I don't know what to do," don't immediately assume the role of *Change Agent*. You'll only confront a brick wall of frustration and the other person's inability to make changes. Your role as *Consultant* is the clear choice. Its purpose is to help your partner look objectively at the concerns that are blocking his or her progress. First use an identity meditation to silently affirm confidence in your ability to counsel your partner. Now help your partner clarify goals by creatively analyzing the situation. For example, break up the problem into pieces and conduct a SWOT analysis (see Chapter Five).

A SWOT analysis helps you discover the other person's weaknesses and strengths and reveals any barriers to success that the outside environment might be posing.

Pitchman/Pitchwoman

There's a time and a place and subtle strategies that can be used to pitch ideas or products. Most people don't come by that knowledge and skill naturally. However, the role of *Pitchman or Pitchwoman* is learnable. Getting to that "yes" of adoption, however, will involve some hefty self-talk and an effective identity meditation that you may need to repeat silently during the pitch. Your task? To discover and dismantle the other person's fears and hot-button issues while meeting his or her needs at the same time. Make sure to employ the communication strategies known to work; for example, use motivational words such as "*right now*," awaken anticipatory regret in the other person if he or she backs off from buying into the situation, parry objections with factual information, and reframe the situation in terms of the benefits meaningful to him or her.

Ally

Compassion, insight, and a degree of selflessness will help you be an *Ally*, stepping up to the plate to help another person to stay in focus and stay the course. An *Ally* should be prepared to take some personal risks; sometimes those risks involve your job and sometimes your social standing. As an *Ally*, you're part relationships artist, part investigator. You draw on your own experiences and applying what you've learned to your partner's situation. You discover the arguments behind opposing interests and marshal the facts and logic to counter them. You design the action to be taken. Remember that the *Ally* role is not adversarial: Your purpose is to defend and support, and both of these actions will build trust in the relationship.

Friend

The final role, *Friend,* can't be dismissed lightly: It carries both commitment and responsibility. To be a *Friend* means to go the extra mile, to stand up for your partner, but to do both without compromising your own values and ideas. These days, workplace friendships are highly valued by some organizations because they increase productivity and promote employee retention; other organizations view them as time-wasters. Nevertheless, as a *Friend* you should be supportive and accepting of the other person and able to show genuine affection and empathy. Part of your role is to champion your partner to others and to both challenge and stimulate him or her to succeed. Remember to establish boundaries in the friendship and to avoid breaching your partner's privacy by making comments you know would not be welcomed.

Moving from one role to another

The role you assume at any given moment is the one cued by the other person. You want your action in that role to be genuine and effective. However, that depends on your existing relationship with the other person and the amount of flexibility within it. Don't anticipate transitioning quickly among roles; mistakes can be made that way. But do remember the purpose for assuming other roles: to meet the needs of the other person as well as your own. Pre-plan how you're going to handle yourself in the other roles; gauge the other person's reaction by mentally rehearsing the roles.

Make sure to evoke an identity meditation before assuming each role and to follow your intuition. Remember that success ultimately depends on your flexibility to transition roles and to temporarily relinquish your desired one.

Matching up communication styles and personality types

A word, a grunt, a jittery gaze or limp handshake—communication is a mixed bag of verbal, vocal, and nonverbal cues. Faulty communication—the inconsistency of an insincere smile accompanied by a firm handshake, for example—can destroy your intent. Listen to the other person. Your good listening behavior can make the difference in achieving your goal or failing in it. Validate what he or she says to you by summarizing and feeding it back appropriately. This continues the dialogue by establishing a connection between the two of you.

In any role you assume in negotiation, it's essential to modify your communication style to the other person's personality type. By heeding personality types (see Chapter Ten), you'll become role-adaptable to different situations and different people; this leverages the influence you'll have in transitioning between roles and helps in motivating, teaching, and leading others.

A powerful dynamic

The role system dynamic is powerful. These series of relationship strategies are proven to take you well beyond "*Yes*" as they influence others to change perspective. First, set a goal for your influence. Pre-plan the strategies and tactics you'll need to reach it, matching your choice to the personality preference of the other person. Plan also for transitioning between roles, the ones you may have to assume before reaching your final one. Be adaptable, ready to assume roles based on the cues you receive from the other person. If you follow this procedure throughout the role sequencing and stay on task, you'll not only meet your goal but will be equipped to handle any influence challenge.

Go for it!